BETSY ROSS

DISCOVER THE LIFE OF AN AMERICAN LEGEND

David and Patricia Armentrout

Rourke
Publishing LLC
Vero Beach, Florida 32964

www.rourkepublishing.com

PHOTO CREDITS: © Armentrout: page 4; © PhotoDisc: page 7; © Courtesy Betsy Ross House, Philadelphia: page 21; © Visual Information Support Center, United States National Guard, Nashville, Tennessee: page 10; © Library of Congress: Cover, Title page, pages 8, 12, 15, 17, 18

Cover: *Betsy Ross-American seamstress*
Title page : *The birth of "Old Glory"*

Editor: Frank Sloan

Cover design by Nicola Stratford

Library of Congress Cataloging-in-Publication Data

Armentrout, David, 1962-
Betsy Ross / David and Patricia Armentrout.
    v. cm. — (Discover the life of an American legend)
Includes bibliographical references and index.
Contents: The American Flag — Betsy Ross — Betsy marries — The Grand
Union Flag — George Washington visits Philadelphia — The "Stars and Stripes" —Betsy sews for the Navy
— Betsy's family — The Betsy Ross house — Dates to remember.
    ISBN 1-58952-661-9 (hardcover)
    1. Ross, Betsy, 1752-1836—Juvenile literature. 2. Revolutionaries—United States—Biography—Juvenile
literature. 3. United States—History—Revolution, 1775-1783—Flags—Juvenile literature. 4. Flags—United
States—History—18th century—Juvenile literature. [1. Ross, Betsy, 1752-1836. 2. Revolutionaries. 3.
Flags--United States. 4. Women--Biography.] I. Armentrout, Patricia,
1960- II. Title. III. Series.
    E302.6.R77A76 2003
    973.3'092--dc21

                                                        2003002206

Printed in the USA

CG/CG

Table of Contents

The American Flag

The American flag is a **symbol** of liberty and freedom to millions of Americans.

No one knows for sure who made the first American flag. Many people believe Betsy Ross sewed the first flag. The story of Betsy Ross and the flag is a **legend**. A legend is a story based on fact that may, or may not, be true.

Students raise the American flag at their school each morning.

Betsy Ross

Betsy Ross was born Elizabeth Griscom in 1752. Elizabeth was nicknamed Betsy. She grew up in Philadelphia, which was the capital of the colonies during the **American Revolution.**

Betsy's father was a carpenter. He helped build the bell tower at Independence Hall, where the Declaration of Independence was adopted and signed.

Construction of Independence Hall began in 1730.

Betsy Marries

When Betsy grew up she worked in a sewing shop. There she met John Ross. They married in 1773 and started a sewing business of their own.

In 1775, a group of **patriots**, including George Washington and Benjamin Franklin, met to talk about the Revolutionary War. They also discussed a flag design for the **Continental Army**.

Benjamin Franklin helped draft the Declaration of Independence.

The Grand Union Flag

On January 1, 1776 the Grand Union Flag was raised for the first time. The banner had 13 alternating red and white stripes with the British flag in the upper left corner. The Grand Union represented the Continental Army's fight for freedom.

Meanwhile, the sewing business was slow, so John Ross joined the Pennsylvania **militia**. He was hurt in an explosion and died from his wounds.

George Washington Visits Philadelphia

As the Revolutionary War continued, patriots grew tired of the Grand Union Flag. They no longer wanted a British symbol on their banner. Once again a new flag was desired.

George Washington was the commander of the Continental Army. According to legend, he visited Betsy's sewing shop. Washington showed Betsy a sketch of what he wanted the new flag to look like.

George Washington commanded the Continental Army before becoming the first United States president.

The "Stars and Stripes"

As the story goes, Washington wanted 13 stripes on the new flag. He also wanted 13 stars, arranged in a circle, to represent the original 13 colonies. Betsy suggested that the stars should have five points. Within a few days Betsy completed the first official American flag.

George Washington, Betsy Ross, and the first American flag

Betsy Sews for the Navy

Betsy continued to work in her shop and helped the Pennsylvania navy by sewing flags for their ships.

In 1777, Betsy married Joseph Ashburn. They later had two children. Joseph was a captain in the Continental Army. His boat was captured by the British during a trip for supplies. Joseph was put in prison and died there in 1782.

Many prisoners died while being held captive on British prison ships.

Betsy's Family

Betsy married again in 1783. Betsy and her husband John Claypoole had five daughters. John died in 1817.

Betsy continued to work until the age of 75. Betsy died in 1836 at the age of 84.

Betsy's daughters, nieces, and grandson said Betsy often told them the story about how she designed and sewed the first American flag.

Betsy cuts and sews stars for the new American flag.

The Betsy Ross House

We may never know if Betsy Ross made the first American Flag. However, The Betsy Ross House in Philadelphia is considered the birthplace of the American flag. It remains a popular tourist attraction.

The historic Betsy Ross House in Philadelphia

Dates to Remember

1752	Born January 1 in Philadelphia
1773	Betsy marries John Ross
1776	John Ross dies
1776	Betsy meets with George Washington
1776	Betsy sews the American flag
1777	Betsy marries Joseph Ashburn
1782	Joseph Ashburn dies
1783	Betsy marries John Claypoole
1817	John Claypoole dies
1836	Betsy dies at the age of 84

Glossary

American Revolution (uh MAIR uh kuhn rev uh LOO shuhn) — The war that lasted from 1775 to 1783 in which the 13 American colonies won their independence from Great Britain

Continental Army (kon tuh NEN tul ARE mee) — troops made up of American colonists who fought against the British in the American Revolutionary War

legend (LEDG uhnd) — a story, which may or may not be true, based on fact

militia (muh LISH uh) — a group of citizens who are trained to fight, but not as part of a regular army

patriots (PAY tree uts) — people who love their country and are prepared to fight for it

symbol (SIM buhl) — something that stands for something else

Index

Further Reading

Ferry, Joseph. *The American Flag*. Mason Crest Publishers, 2003
Greene, Stephanie. *Betsy Ross and the Silver Thimble*. Aladdin, 2002
Roop, Connie. *Betsy Ross*. Scholastic, 2002

Websites To Visit

www.ushistory.org/betsy/
www.usflag.org/about.betsy.ross.html
womenshistory.about.com/library/bio/blross.htm

About The Authors

David and Patricia Armentrout have written many nonfiction books for young readers. They specialize in science and social studies topics. They have had several books published for primary school reading. The Armentrouts live in Cincinnati, Ohio, with their two children.